**This book is to be returned on or before
the last date stamped below.**

THIS WALKER BOOK BELONGS TO:

_____

_____

_____

_____

About Turtles

Sea turtles are related
to tortoises and terrapins.
They are all reptiles.

Sea turtles are great wanderers,
travelling thousands of miles
each year, often far from land.
This makes them difficult to
study. So scientists are only just
beginning to find out about
their mysterious lives.

There are seven species of sea
turtle. This book is about the
Loggerhead turtle. Loggerheads
live in seas all over the world.

For Joseph and Gabriel,
Zoe and Finnian
N.D.

For Auntie Sam, our tortoise-sitter
J.C.

With thanks to Daniel R. Evans
Sea Turtle Survival League Education Coordinator
Caribbean Conservation Corporation
http://www.cccturtle.org

First published 2001 by Walker Books Ltd
87 Vauxhall Walk, London SE11 5HJ

This edition published 2002

2 4 6 8 10 9 7 5 3 1

Text © 2001 Nicola Davies Illustrations © 2001 Jane Chapman

This book has been typeset in Goldentype

Printed in Hong Kong

British Library Cataloguing in Publication Data: a catalogue record
for this book is available from the British Library

ISBN 0-7445-9401-4

One Tiny TURTLE

Nicola Davies

Illustrated by Jane Chapman

WALKER BOOKS
AND SUBSIDIARIES
LONDON · BOSTON · SYDNEY

Far, far out to sea,
land is only a memory, and
empty sky touches the water.

Just beneath the surface
is a tangle of weed and driftwood
where tiny creatures cling.
This is the nursery of a sea turtle.

Passing in a boat,
you might not notice Turtle.
Not much bigger than a bottle top,
she hides in the green shadows.

She's a baby, so her shell is soft as old leather.
Just a little fish bite could rip it open.
But Turtle is safe in her world of weed,
and snaps her beak on tiny crabs
and shrimps.

Turtles have a shell covering their backs and one covering their tummies.
The shells are made from bony plates which get bigger
and harder as the turtle grows.

Turtle swims about,
flapping her long front flippers
like wings: she is underwater flying.

She pokes her pin-prick nostrils
through the silver surface
to take a swift breath –
so fast, blink and you'd miss it!

Fish breathe underwater, but turtles are reptiles
and need to come up to the surface for air.
They do this every four to five minutes when they are active.
When they are asleep, they can stay underwater for hours.

Then she's gone,
diving down into
her secret life again.

For three or four years,
maybe more, Turtle
rides out the storms,

and floats through
the hot calms.

Steadily she outgrows her nursery.

Nobody sees her leave,
but when you look for her,
she has vanished all the same.

A year or two later she turns up close to land.
Bigger than a dinner plate now,
she's not a fish snack any more.
Her shell is hard as armour,
her head is tough as a helmet.
She's grown into her name: Loggerhead.

She has come to eat crabs.
Millions swim up from deep water
to breed in the shallows.
Their shells crack as easily as
hens' eggs in her heavy jaws.
But in a week the feast is over
and Loggerhead disappears again.

Loggerhead wanders far and wide
in search of food:

in summer, to cool seaweed jungles, where
she finds juicy clams and shoals of shrimps.

And in winter, to turquoise lagoons, warm as
a bath, where she can munch among corals.

Loggerhead may travel thousands of miles, but
she leaves no trace or track for you to follow.
Only good luck will catch you a glimpse of her.

For thirty years you might not find her.
Then one summer night here she is,
on the beach where she was born.
She's found her way here, sensing north
and south like a compass needle, feeling
the current and the warmth of the waves.
She remembers the taste of the water
here, and the sound of the surf.

Male turtles wait just off the nesting beaches.
They mate with the females
before they come ashore to lay eggs.

Loggerhead has grown in her wandering years.

She's big as a barrow now.

Floating in the sea she weighs nothing,

but on land she's heavier than a man.

So every flipper step is a struggle,

and her eyes stream with salty tears,

which help keep them free of sand.

Coming ashore is very risky for sea turtles – they can easily overheat and die. So they only nest at night or in cooler weather. Then they get back to the sea as soon as possible.

Loggerhead makes
her nest where the
sea won't reach.

Scooping carefully with
her hind flippers ...

she makes a steep, deep hole.

Inside she lays her eggs,
like a hundred squidgy ping-pong balls.

Afterwards she covers them with sand
to hide her nest from hungry mouths.

Then Loggerhead is gone again,
back to her secret life.

Left behind, under the sand, her eggs stay
deep and safe. Baby turtles grow inside.

Females stay close to their nesting beach for several months.
In that time they usually make at least four nests,
and sometimes as many as ten.

And before
the summer's over
they wriggle from
their shells.

Turtle eggs in warm sand can be ready to hatch in six weeks. If the sand is cool, they can take three weeks longer.

Above them on the beach a hundred eyes watch,
on the lookout for a meal.
So the hatchlings wait until night.

The horizon where the sea meets the sky tells baby turtles which way to turn to get to the water. But street lights and buildings next to the beach can confuse them and make them go the wrong way.

Then they burst through the sand and skeeter towards the sea.

In the dark, claws and beaks
and grabbing paws
miss just one young turtle.
One day, she'll remember this beach
and come back.

But now she dives under the waves and swims.
Swims and swims!
Out into the arms of the ocean.
Far, far out to sea, land becomes a memory
waiting to wake in the head of the little turtle.

INDEX

Look up the pages
to find out about all
of these turtle things.
Don't forget to look at
both kinds of word –

this kind
and
this kind.

About the Author

Nicola Davies has loved turtles ever since she first saw one in the middle of the Indian Ocean. But people are eating their eggs, building on their beaches, polluting their seas. She wrote this book to show that turtles are precious and deserve more care. Nicola is also the author of *Big Blue Whale*, *Bat Loves the Night* and *Wild About Dolphins*.

About the Illustrator

Jane Chapman loves turtles, too, and her own 75-year-old pet tortoise inspired her paintings. Jane's other books for Walker include *The Emperor's Egg* (Winner of the TES Junior Information Book Award) by Martin Jenkins, and *One Duck Stuck* by Phyllis Root.

NOTES FOR TEACHERS

The READ AND WONDER series is an innovative and versatile resource for reading, thinking and discovery. Each book invites children to become excited about a topic, see how varied information books can be, and want to find out more.

Reading aloud The story form makes these books ideal for reading aloud – in their own right or as part of a cross-curricular topic, to a child or to a whole class. After you've introduced children to the books in this way, they can revisit and enjoy them again and again.

Shared reading Big Book editions are available for several titles, so children can read along, discuss the topic, and comment on the different ways information is presented – to wonder together.

Group and guided reading Children need to experience a range of reading materials. Information books like these help develop the skills of reading to learn, as part of learning to read. With the support of a reading group, children can become confident, flexible readers.

Paired reading It's fun to take turns to read the information in the main text or captions. With a partner, children can explore the pages to satisfy their curiosity and build their understanding.

Individual reading These books can be read for interest and pleasure by children at home and in school.

Research Once children have been introduced to these books through reading aloud, they can use them for independent or group research, as part of a curricular topic.

Children's own writing You can offer these books as strong models for children's own information writing. They can record their observations and findings about a topic, make field notes and sketches, and add extra snippets of information for the reader.

Above all, Read and Wonders are to be enjoyed, and encourage children to develop a lasting curiosity about the world they live in.

Sue Ellis, Centre for Language in Primary Education